THE NIGHT
and Other
Amazing Sights in Space

Stars and Constellations

Nick Hunter

Heinemann
LIBRARY

Chicago, Illinois

Edited by Rebecca Rissman, Daniel Nunn,
and Sian Smith
Designed by Joanna Hinton-Malivoire and Marcus Bell
Picture research by Mica Brancic
Production by Sophia Argyris
Originated by Capstone Global Library Ltd
Printed in the United States of America in
North Mankato, Minnesota

122013
007930RP

Library of Congress Cataloging-in-Publication Data
Hunter, Nick.
  Stars and constellations / Nick Hunter.—1st ed.
      p. cm.—(The night sky: and other amazing sights)
Includes bibliographical references and index.

ISBN 978-1-4329-7517-3 (hb)
ISBN 978-1-4329-7522-7 (pb)

1. Stars—Juvenile literature. 2. Sun—Juvenile literature.
3. Constellations—Juvenile literature. I. Title.

  QB801.7.H86 2014

  523.8—dc23   2012043049

Acknowledgments
The author and publisher are grateful to the following
for permission to reproduce copyright material: Alamy
p.25 (© The Art Gallery Collection); British Library
p.24 (©The British Library Board); Getty Images p.28
(Science Photo Library/Eckhard Slawik); NASA pp.9,
18, 10 (SDO), 11 (Visible Earth/EOS Project Science
Office/Goddard Space Flight Center), 13 (ESA, M.
Robberto (Space Telescope Science Institute/ESA) and
the Hubble Space Telescope Orion Treasury Project
Team), 14 (JAXA), 15 (ESA/Johns Hopkins University),
19 (JPL-Caltech/ESA/Harvard-Smithsonian CfA), 20
(Hubble Space Telescope), 22 (ESA/SOHO); Rex
Features p.21 (Charles Brewer); Science Photo Library
pp.5 (European Southern Observatory), 6, 17 (Babak
Tafreshi, TWAN), 7 (Roger Harris), 16 (David Nunuk), 23
(Julian Baum), 26 (Eckhard Slawik), 27 (Ben Canales),
29 (Luke Dodd); Shutterstock pp.4 (© fotosutra.com),
8 (© Werner Buchel); WIYN and NOAO/AURA/NSF//
University of Alaska Anchorage/T. A. Rector p12.

Cover photograph of the constellation the Great
Bear reproduced with permission of Shutterstock (©
ella1977).

We would like to thank Stuart Atkinson for his invaluable
help in the preparation of this book.

Every effort has been made to contact copyright
holders of any material reproduced in this book. Any
omissions will be rectified in subsequent printings if
notice is given to the publisher.

Contents

Some words are shown in bold, **like this**. You can find them in the glossary on page 30.

Out of This World

There are thousands of twinkling lights in the sky. Most of these tiny dots are stars. They are far bigger than **planet** Earth, where we live.

You can see different stars depending on what time of year it is.

The light from these distant stars takes 50 million years to reach Earth.

The stars look like tiny lights because they are very far away from Earth. The light from the farthest stars we can see takes millions of years to reach Earth.

What Are Stars?

Stars are huge balls of burning gases. They are incredibly hot. Many things that travel too close to stars are destroyed immediately.

Sirius

Sirius is the brightest star in the night sky.

White stars are hotter than yellow or red stars.

Not all stars are the same. Stars in the sky can glow red, yellow, or white. Stars can also be very different in size.

Our Own Star

The closest star to Earth is the Sun. All heat and light on Earth comes from the Sun. Plants need sunlight to grow. People and animals eat plants.

Sunflowers turn toward the heat of the Sun.

The Sun is about 93 million miles (150 million kilometers) from Earth.

The Sun is much bigger than Earth. It is not as big as some other stars. However, it is closer to Earth than any other star, so it appears very bright to us.

What Makes Stars Shine?

Stars are mostly made of a material called **hydrogen**. Stars make heat and light from **reactions** going on deep inside them. The heat and light created by the reactions move through space to Earth and other **planets**.

The surface of a star is cooler than the middle, where the reactions happen.

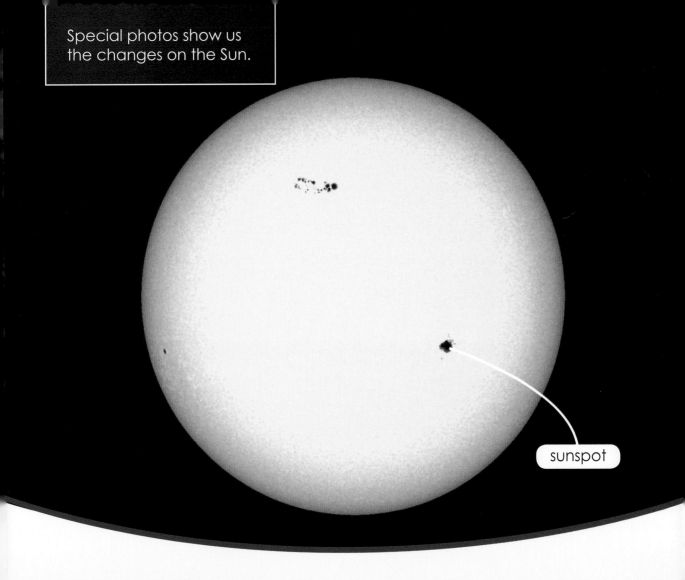

Special photos show us the changes on the Sun.

sunspot

The surface of a star is always changing. **Sunspots** are cooler areas on the Sun's surface. Sunspots on the Sun's surface seem small, but they can actually be thousands of miles wide.

Where Do Stars Come From?

Stars form in giant clouds of gas and dust called **nebulas**. Over millions of years, the force of **gravity** pulls the tiny **particles** of the cloud together.

Light from the Rosette Nebula takes about 5,000 years to reach Earth.

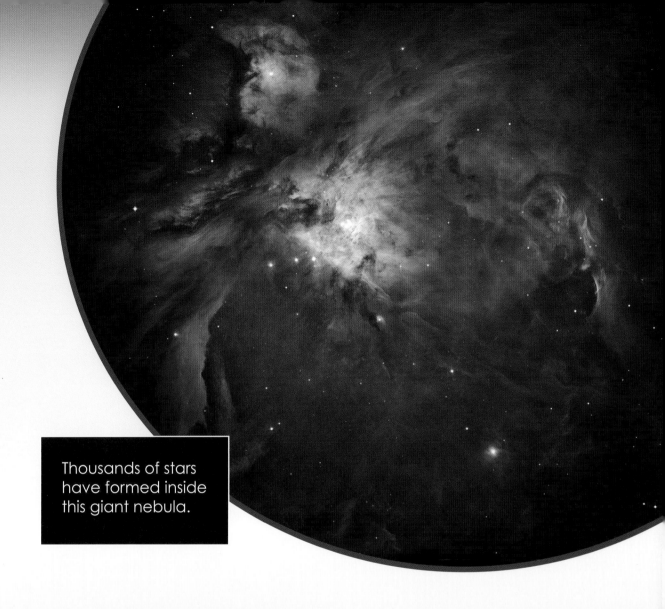

Thousands of stars have formed inside this giant nebula.

The gas and dust heat up as they come together. The cloud becomes so big and hot that **reactions** start up deep inside. They release heat and light. A new star is born.

Do Stars Last Forever?

Stars change over billions of years. The Sun is an ordinary yellow star. A very long time from now, the Sun will become a huge red giant star. It will then shrink again as its fuel finally runs out.

This picture shows what the Sun could look like when it becomes a red giant star.

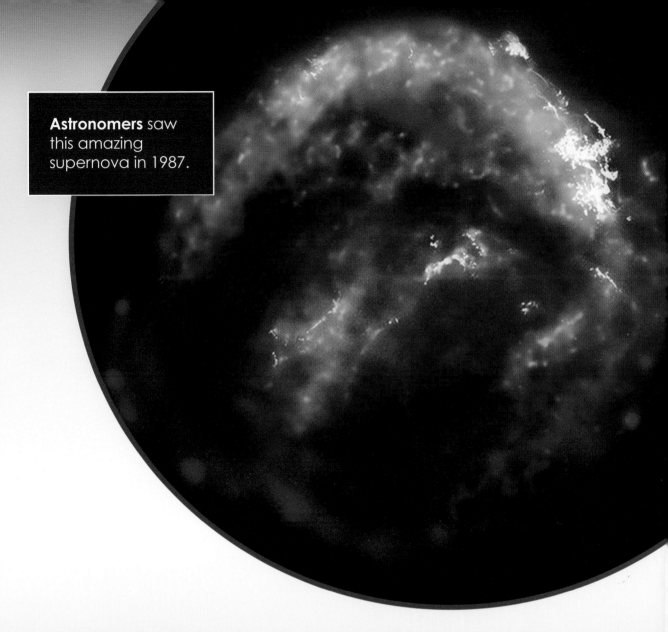

Astronomers saw this amazing supernova in 1987.

The biggest stars end in a big bang. This is called a **supernova**. The **reactions** in the star happen so fast that the whole star explodes.

15

Constellations

Ancient people gave names to the groups of stars that formed patterns or shapes. We call these groups **constellations**. We still use them to map the night sky.

Different constellations can be seen in each season of the year.

Drawings have been added to this photograph. They show the shape of two constellations, Orion and the Big Dog.

The ancient Greeks named this constellation Orion. Orion was a giant hunter in Greek stories. The Greeks thought the three bright stars in the middle looked like Orion's belt.

Across the Universe

There are billions of different stars in the **universe**. Sometimes, two stars close together will **orbit**, or move around, each other. These are called double, or binary, stars.

This double star is named Albireo.

The spiral shape of the M81 galaxy is very similar to the Milky Way galaxy.

Billions of stars can be grouped together in a **galaxy**. The Sun is part of the Milky Way galaxy. Galaxies come in different shapes and sizes, too.

Exploring Stars

Astronomers study the stars. They use powerful **telescopes** to see across space. No one knows how many stars there are. Distant **galaxies** contain billions of stars that we cannot see from Earth.

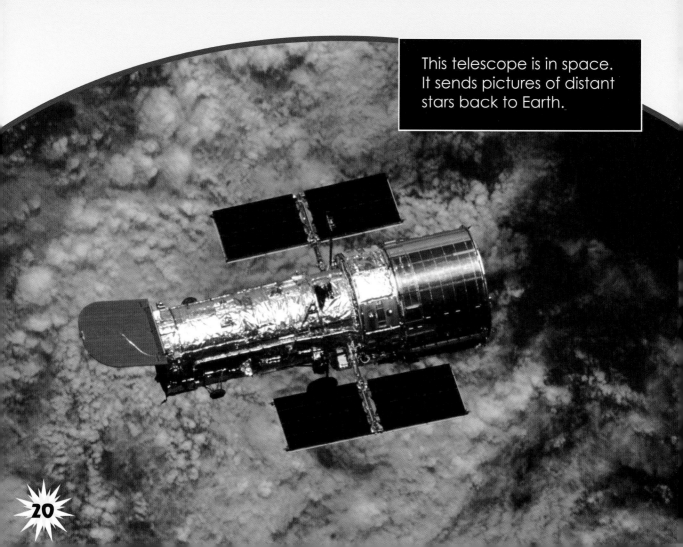

This telescope is in space. It sends pictures of distant stars back to Earth.

Radio telescopes like this one help astronomers find out about how stars formed.

All stars release **energy**. Radio telescopes can pick up this energy even if the stars or galaxies are too far away to see. Astronomers are still finding out new secrets of the stars.

Visiting the Stars

Stars are far too hot for any person or **spacecraft** to visit. However, scientists have launched spacecraft that **orbit** around the Sun. They collect information about how the star is changing.

This spacecraft is being used to study the Sun.

Proxima Centauri

Proxima Centauri is actually the smallest of three stars that are grouped together.

Other stars are a very long way away. After the Sun, the next closest star to Earth is Proxima Centauri. It takes four years for the light from this star to reach us.

Beliefs of the Past

Ancient people believed that the Sun and other stars moved around Earth. They thought the stars were lights attached to the sky. We now know that Earth moves around the Sun.

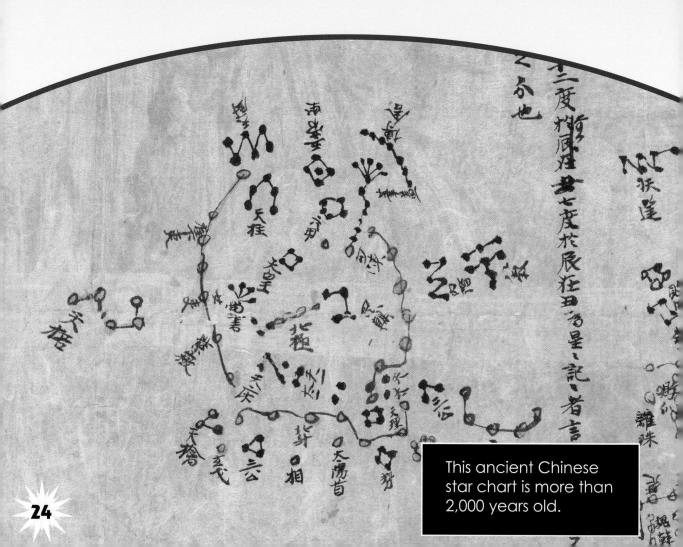

This ancient Chinese star chart is more than 2,000 years old.

Ancient sailors knew that the constellations appeared in different parts of the sky, depending on where they sailed.

Constellations were not just patterns in the sky. Sailors could use the positions of constellations to tell the location of their ships at sea.

See for Yourself

On a clear night, you can see lots of stars in the sky. Look for Polaris, also called the North Star or Pole Star. This star can be seen over the North Pole from the United States and Canada.

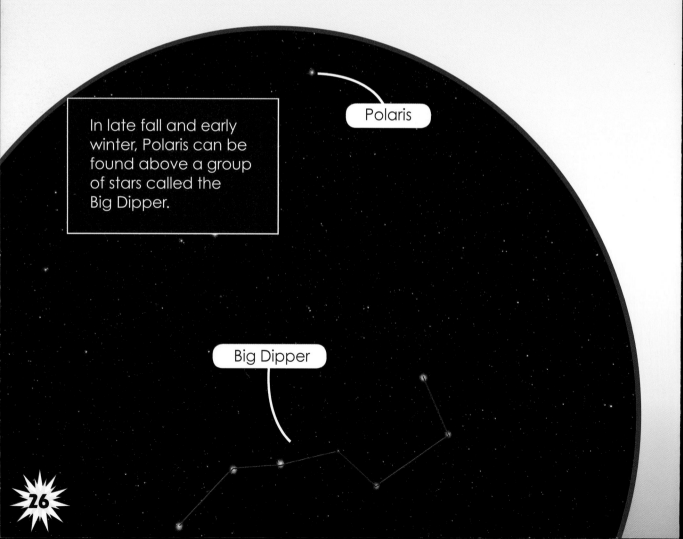

In late fall and early winter, Polaris can be found above a group of stars called the Big Dipper.

Polaris

Big Dipper

Before looking at the stars, sit in the dark for a while so your eyes can adjust.

For real stargazing, you'll want to look through a **telescope** or **binoculars**. This will make the stars look clearer. You'll see more from a dark place, away from brightly lit cities and roads.

Finding Constellations

See if you can find these **constellations** in the sky.

- The Big Dipper is shown on page 26. It is part of a constellation called Ursa Major, or the Great Bear.
- Cassiopeia (below) looks like the letter "W" or the letter "M," depending on when and where you see it.

Cassiopeia is named after a queen from ancient Greek stories.

- Orion the Hunter is shown on page 17. It can be seen from northern and southern countries.
- Crux (below) is one of the best constellations to look for in southern countries such as Australia and South Africa.

Crux, or the Southern Cross, is shown on the flag of Australia.

Glossary

astronomer person who studies space and the night sky

binoculars device used to look at things that are far away

constellation pattern or group of stars in the night sky

energy power. Heat and light are forms of energy.

galaxy huge collection of stars, gas, and dust

gravity force that pulls all objects together and is usually only felt from large objects such as stars and planets

hydrogen substance from which the Sun is made and that reacts to release energy

nebula cloud of gas and dust from which stars and planets form

orbit path that an object in space takes as it moves around another object, such as when Earth goes around the Sun; also the act of moving along that path

particle tiniest possible piece of a material

planet large object (usually made of rock or gas) that orbits a star. Our planet, Earth, goes around the Sun.

reaction when chemicals or materials change

spacecraft object made by humans that travels into space

sunspot cooler, dark patch on the Sun

supernova huge explosion of a dying star

telescope device used to make things in space look bigger

universe everything in space, including Earth and millions of stars and planets

Find Out More

Books

Bingham, Caroline. *First Space Encyclopedia*. New York: DK Children, 2008.

Sasaki, Chris, and Alan Flinn. *Constellations: A Glow-in-the-Dark Guide to the Night Sky*. New York: Sterling, 2006.

Than, Ker. *Stars* (True Books: Space). Danbury, Conn.: Children's Press, 2010.

Thomas, Isabel. *Stars and Galaxies* (Astronaut Travel Guides). Chicago: Raintree, 2012.

Web sites

Facthound offers a safe, fun way to find Internet sites related to this book. All of the sites on Facthound have been researched by our staff.

Here's all you do:

Visit **www.facthound.com**

Type in this code: 9781432975173

Index